TWO GEMS FROM RUDOLF STEINER

Two lectures from 1904 & 1905, on clairvoyance and the initiatory quest, from unpublished archive records.

Lectures in Berlin from 30th October, 1904
and 16th October, 1905

Restored, edited and translated by

Adrian Anderson   Ph.D

Also available by this author:

The Rudolf Steiner Handbook
The Foundation Stone Meditation: a new commentary
The Way to the Sacred
Living a Spiritual year: seasonal festivals
The Hellenistic Mysteries & Christianity
Dramatic anthroposophy: identification and contextualization of
  primary features of Rudolf Steiner's anthroposophy. (A Ph.D. thesis)

see www.rudolfsteinerstudies.com for further publications

(c) 2011   The author asserts the moral right to be regarded as the originator of this book

(c) 2011 The English translation of the lectures here are copyright to the author.
Threshold Publishing, Australia

ISBN 978-0-9941602-1-8

Clairvoyance:
or perceiving what one journeys through in spiritual realms during the night

translated and edited by Dr. Adrian Anderson

A previously unpublished lecture by Rudolf Steiner to members of Theosophical Society, given on 30th October 1904, in Berlin.

Translator-editor's Preface:

Only late in the 20th century were notes of this lecture discovered. It had been assumed for decades that none existed. I was fortunate to acquire a copy of the now 110-year-old manuscript in Germany in 1982. It is in a very dilapidated condition and required painstaking work to reconstruct. This is one of the earlier lectures by Rudolf Steiner, given not long after he had been appointed General Secretary of the German Branch of the Theosophical Society. The word 'theosophy' in this context however refers to his own high initiate knowledge, later called 'anthroposophy'. He was only at the beginning of his teaching mission in 1904. In the years following he was to provide a wealth of new, much more detailed and contemporary meditative texts and advice.

The notes are somewhat abridged, and as this is a very early lecture of his, some references need to be clarified. I have therefore added words in the body of text in various places to clarify the meaning. Additional words from me, needed to complete a sentence are in brackets but note this does not indicate emphasis, but rather a clarifying addition. Furthermore there is also various extensive explanatory material of mine in brackets, but also in italics {*like this*}. Moreover an asterisk (*) indicates that the sentence or phrase, in the original manuscript is too unclear to allow a definite translation.

Antiquated language which today may appear sexist or odd has been updated, for example the term, 'esotericism' is used to replace 'occultism', which now has a negative connotation. I have used the term 'meditant' instead of the term 'the person', to remind the reader that it is through meditating that the higher experiences referred to here are reached.

Also where the German text has the neutral word 'Mensch' which translates as 'man', but actually means the human being, I have used either the phrase 'he or she' / 'she or he', or 'his or her', to reflect the inclusive nature of the German term.

My book, the Rudolf Steiner Handbook, provides a clear and comprehensive guide to the many aspects of anthroposophy that these lectures draw on.

Lecture:
No genuine esotericist will fail to recognise the great danger that could arise if esoteric knowledge were to be popularised in an irresponsible manner. Such activity would cause harm. On the other side we must also take into consideration that Theosophy places on us the duty to represent and spread certain esoteric truths, namely truths that can only derive from esoteric experiences. If one does this, then indeed those people who listen to such teachings will also feel a need to know something of the method whereby such insights can be attained.

Our theoretical books speak of the development of humanity; they speak of the development of the Earth, that is of its cultural epochs and time cycles, and of the planetary systems and other matters. Those who hear much about such themes shall at some time feel the need to ask what kind of {inner} path leads to the experiencing of such truths. They will feel this need even if they strongly accept that these truths can be illumined by the ordinary intelligence. Now in general it is not easy to speak about this path.

But today I do want to make some observations about the potential abilities of the individual through which a person may be led to their own experiences; experiences of their own which can give them conviction of the truth behind theosophical teachings. I wish firstly to consider the nature of what the esotericist calls clairvoyance. In doing this, I am not confusing Theosophy with actual esoteric experiences. Theosophy is basically and simply the formulated expression of the experiences which can be undergone in esoteric experience. {*He later used the term 'Anthroposophy' which is the actual experienced spiritual wisdom, and the term 'Spiritual Science' for the research, carried out in accordance with scientific methodology, which becomes the formulated expression of this wisdom.*}

Practical esotericism is the source of Theosophy. Allow me to speak of a small chapter of this esotericism. The experiences that lie at the foundation of theosophical teachings are undertaken in a different consciousness condition to that which is the normal state of the average human being. Today we will consider at first two such states, and I wish to describe these a little. Let us proceed from what the ordinary human being experiences. The ordinary human being has its daily 'awake' state; namely that state through which is perceived around one the things in the sense world. Further in this state one is able to understand through the intellect, cause and effect, and one is also able to explain the underlying dynamics involved in this world.

This consciousness state is not the only mode for experiencing the world that the ordinary human being can have. Human experience extends far beyond that which is accessible to its consciousness. The normal human being already has two other states of consciousness, *{making three states in all. In addition to the daytime awake state there also exists, secondly,}* the dream state, which is sleep permeated with dreams. Thirdly there is the state of dreamless sleep.

Now you all know that the second state, sleeping, which is permeated by dreams, does not place a human being entirely into unconsciousness. A person is able to bring something of the dream world over into waking consciousness. That which one does bring over in this way is not the content of the actual experience that was undergone during the dreaming-sleep phase in the spiritual worlds. The experience is something different from that of which one later becomes conscious, that is, in the form of a dream.

The dream is only a bringing over to consciousness some fragments, some reflex pictures, of reflected images; it is not the complete and integrated reflected image of what you experienced. It is really just fragmentary images of that which the person underwent in an entirely different world, during the dreaming-sleep phase, as distinct from the dreamless-sleep phase. During the actual experience the contents are integrated and coherent, it is from these realities, which one does indeed experience there, one has some recollections, namely dreams.

{A dream is in fact what we recall of our night-time experiences. It is some memories of the realities that we encountered, but of which we are not really conscious; hence we have only a memory image of it.}

The dreamer has upon awakening brought these images over into the memory for the awake consciousness, and one thereby remembers the experience. But the content of the actual experience is only sparsely remembered, and is recalled in a distorted way. It thus becomes a memory that cannot be compared in any way with what one actually has experienced over there. What is experienced over there is a world that if it could be really consciously observed, is seen to be filled with things of the astral world, just as our physical world is filled with things of a material nature. Over there we encounter physical reality just as we do here, but we experience the inner side of normal physical reality when we are in the astral realm. In particular we directly encounter human emotions over there.

{*This awareness in the astral world is the second state of awareness that is possible, the first being physical-plane day-consciousness. That is to say, if the meditant were conscious in the astral world, instead of only recalling the journey there, later on, as so-called 'dreams'*}.

Thus we encounter in the soul world, the passions, wishes, desires and lusts from the same events, deriving from the same situations of the physical world. We experience these emotions are they actually are, and not only as they manifest in the form of our personal reality, making its way in and through physical life. It is indeed a different kind of world that the human being experiences there, from which only fragments are brought over into the normal awake condition.

A person should never seek to precisely define an experience occurring on the so-called astral plane just simply from their dreams, for dreams are only a reflection of the original experiences. That is, such a description is simply based on what they bring over in the way of dream contents into their day-wake consciousness. For this astral world is as rich, or rather much richer and more complex world than the sense world.

What this world offers, {*if we can be conscious within it, in the second state of awareness*} with respect to contrasts {of the dynamics} cannot be compared with what occurs in our physical world. There is such a contrast between what appears to you as good and intensely radiant on the one hand, and on the other hand that which appears as terrible, repulsive and awful apparitions. The intense variety of such contrasting appearances cannot be compared with that which our physical world offers.

The third consciousness state is that of dreamless sleep. With the ordinary human being very little of the experiences that it undergoes in dreamless sleep comes across into awake consciousness. Something does actually come across, but usually we do not become aware of it. It does not manifest as something that the usual consciousness assesses as if the person themself had experienced it. Instead the experience of dreamless sleep manifests in waking day-consciousness through exerting an influence, rather than manifesting directly in a causative manner.

For what is actually experienced over there {during dreamless sleep} are the great spiritual laws that govern reality, {*i.e., all the realms of being*}. Such laws are to a certain degree much truer causative factors than those of our physical plane. What actually occurs behind the external physical world of animal and plant kingdoms is experienced over there. These reveal for example how the life there is formed and moulded in these realms themselves, and which great laws actually govern life on Earth.

They reveal how one form develops into existence by metamorphosis from another form: all this the soul goes through, without being able to consciously retain awareness of it in daytime awake-consciousness {*that is when awake back in the body*}. Were these perceptions to penetrate in their real form into usual consciousness, understanding about many factors of life that are otherwise dim and enigmatic would flash into the mind like lightning.

The mineral kingdom does not belong in this connection, for insight about its inner reality can not be perceived during this phase of dreamless sleep. {*Rather, insights are limited to the human, animal and plant realms.*} We have given in these words, a brief description of the three modalities of experience that human beings may have. Of these only one is really a consciousness condition that we encounter in ordinary humanity, namely physical-plane day consciousness.

{*Summing up so far; whilst dreaming the soul is in the astral plane, in dreamless sleep it has journeyed further, into Lower Spirit-land, and thirdly, in deep dreamless sleep, one is in Higher Spirit-land. See diagram opposite.*}

Illustration: This shows the three realms, and what we are journeying through, and could experience, if we were able to have the three stages of awareness during sleep. I have also shown the journey of the soul through the solar system (you can read about this in various Rudolf Steiner lectures on life after death).

THE NIGHT TIME JOURNEY THROUGH THE COSMOS

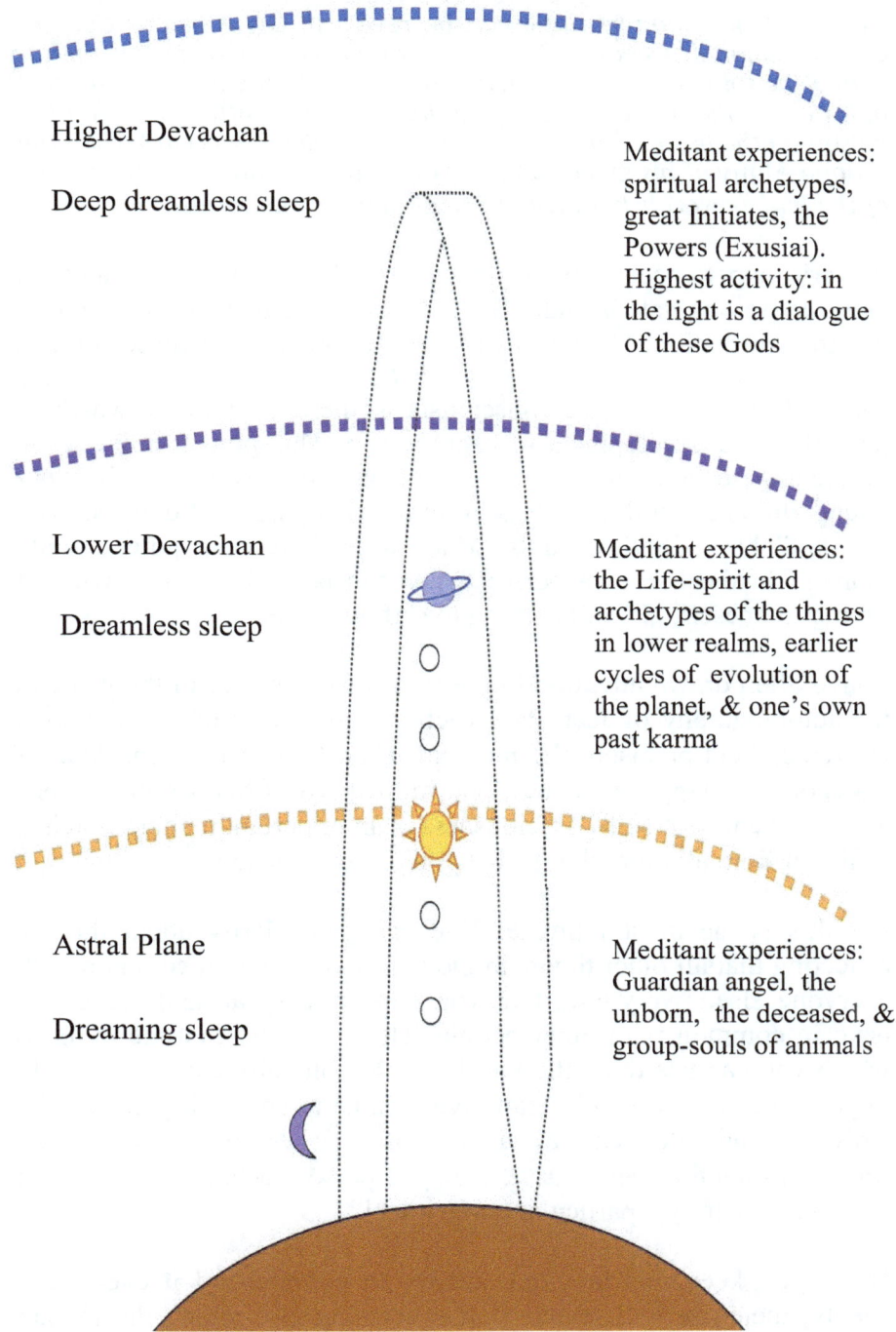

It is obvious that nothing from the experiences which can be achieved in these other states can become the content of esoteric teachings. {*This sentence is ambiguous and means either: until the meditant has personally already begun to understand the essence of such transcendental matters, little can be revealed. Or, it means that the actual personal account of what is experienced there by an initiate cannot be told. This second meaning is more likely, as personal first-hand accounts are regarded by Rudolf Steiner as often "working like poison on the listener" because a sensational element occurs when this is done. Many of his teachings are exactly an elucidation of the nature of the higher worlds but given in clear, impersonal terms.*}

Esoteric experiences only begin when a definite transformation of one's conscious state is under way. Allow me to now describe briefly this transformation; {*he now considers the first state of consciousness, the day-wake kind, one sees that it can become inwardly spiritualized*}. In human consciousness there is a point which is pivotal in the development of each person. This pivotal point is the awakening to self-consciousness. You are all aware that the very young child at first does not speak in the first person; it does not say, "I want" but "Charles wants, Mary wants". It is a quite definite moment in the life of a person when the possibility first arises of saying to oneself, "I", of attaining to self-awareness.

I have often drawn attention to the Berlin friends here of the place in the autobiography of Jean Paul Richter that speaks of this moment. He remembers precisely the moment when he became conscious of his ego. This happened as he stood in the yard of his parents' house. This awakening to self-consciousness is an important matter, which is different from all other things that you can experience.

For this is the most intimate. You can gain clarity about this by reflecting that all other things in the world you have in common with everyone else. Everything that you otherwise speak and name you have in common with other people. There is only this one thing to which you can use this little word, "I". No-one else can ever say "I" to your ego. Everyone else can give a name to something as you do. Only each individual can say "I" to himself or herself, and no-one can say "I" to another ego. Further, only a person, a human being, can designate itself by a particular name, by "I".

When you keep this in mind and try to comprehend it ever more deeply, then you will realize that everything else which the human being can think about, feel, or will, can not be compared with this one fact; that the human being says "I" to itself. Self-consciousness is something exceptionally significant. The thought, the actual concept of the ego is unique and cannot be compared with anything else. Now there is a possibility to address your soul, that is, its thinking capacity, in the same way that you address the ego; namely as essentially yours, as you.

There is a possibility to so educate the ego that just as in usual self-consciousness it is intimate with its own being, it becomes similarly as intimate with its thought-life. In other words, that it forms in this way out of itself its own thought-world. Intimately from the central point of the ego, thoughts can be then conceived and formed, in just the same way that the concept of "I" is formed. If a person becomes able through careful, disciplined meditating, to so relate to his/her own thought-life as the normal person relates only and solely to their ego, then such a meditant is called an intuitive human being. Then in such a person the realm of thoughts proceeds directly out of the centre of their being, they produce other concepts in the same way that they produce the concept of "I".

{*The term, 'intuitive' here should not be confused with Steiner's special use of the term "Intuition", which describes the highest faculty of clairvoyance, which brings awareness of the actual unity of the Self with Deity, through the Hierarchies. See my book, "The Way the Sacred". The term, 'intuitive' here means to be at the first stage of higher awareness, wherein intuition brings an enhanced life into one's thoughts, into one's mind.*}

The thoughts are no longer brain-bound, for they are experienced as they really are in our soul, before they are registered by the brain as images, that is prior to the stage where they are formed into a mental image. Our thoughts have a vital, transcendental holistic quality, but this is rarely experienced, we normally sense only the somewhat sketchy mental image of the thought itself.

I wish to just mention that the theosophical movement has a means with which to reach this meditative separating of the ego. It may seem astonishing, but in the booklet 'Light on the Path' is present the method to attain to this stage of ego-development.

{"Light on the Path" is an extremely valuable meditative guide for meditants given by a high degree Master to an English Theosophist. But note that soon after this lecture, Rudolf Steiner began the process of esoteric teaching, and he gave various meditations to students of his Esoteric School that have the same quality as those in Light on the Path, and indeed are in many respects far more valuable and substantial. These were followed by many other lectures by him over two decades on this subject.}

The stage of ego-development {inferred here} involves conscious persistent meditating in a quite specific sense, through which the person can achieve this stage of representing to themselves their thinking-life as they currently represent their ego. Two sentences in this booklet have the power, when rightly used, to bring the ego to that new standpoint that I have described. They are not abstract sentences, they are sentences that are formulated from millennia of experience of the astral plane. These sentences that have such exceptional transformative powers for the soul are: "Before the eye can see, it must be incapable of tears. Before the ears can hear, they must have lost their sensitivity."

Power and life live in these sentences, they need only be used in the right way. Once the person has attained to this step, then there occurs of necessity something else. That person {i.e., the meditant} is then in the condition wherein he/she may experience in a coherent manner, that which is usually only experienced in dreaming sleep,[1] and which normally only comes over the threshold in fragmentary form as dreams. The person is able to experience this in such a way that this world, which is the astral plane, becomes as real and factual as previously the sense world was.

Two things are then possible, one of which normally precedes the other, as the second is obviously a higher attainment. Namely, as a second step, the esotericist is then able to bring completely across into his awake consciousness that which is experienced in dreaming sleep. Thus he or she retains memory of the realities of the astral plane, or kama-world,[2] this includes the wishes, wants, desires, liking and disliking {*not only of one's own, but also of other beings. This is the second state of awareness*}. Of these realities the meditant now has

---
[1] The manuscript has here 'dreamless sleep' but that is inconsistent, as the next sentence shows.
[2] Kama is a Sanscrit word and means 'desire'.

personal experience, in the same way that the ordinary person has experience of the sense world.

The next, higher phase of this same second state is where the esotericist no longer needs the dreaming sleep. Instead through continual higher development of the intuitive faculty he or she is in the position of viewing this world directly, or one might say, of being attuned to this realm. For then the intuitive thinking consciousness, should the initiate be needing to call upon it, is full of spiritual clarity – there is no longer such thing as arbitrary volition. The expression, "be needing it" is better than the terms that would normally be used, e.g., 'wants' or 'desires', for both these expressions are no longer appropriate here. In this intuitive condition these two types of mental dynamics are united.

The human being also perceives for itself, once it has attained to this state, life's deadly enemy, the dangerous foe of human life and of the closely related nature kingdoms. A foe that basically is always lurking there, always tempting and misleading the human being. This enemy that enters into the human being's astral body, draws the person's wishes and attention away from its spiritual possibilities. This spiritual foe seeks to draw a person away from those possibilities which she or he could perceive through the untainted intellect, according to a person's stage of development and inner abilities. {*That is, a malignant spiritual force that seeks to make the intelligence materialistic, so that we lose sight of spiritual values and goals. These are called the ahrimanic spirits.*}

These opponents of humanity are not less present just because, in normal earthly life, the veil of {material} illusion hides them. These foes of humanity and of the other nature kingdoms are now perceived by the advanced meditant at this stage of conscious perception in the astral plane. For the meditant's further development in esoteric matters this is of immense importance. In this condition, which can be compared to dreaming sleep except that one is being conscious in that phase, the acolyte perceives just what forces are in him/herself that {*deriving from these opposing Powers*} draw one downwards, to lower things. This is in fact the first experience that the acolyte has in this newly attained state of consciousness.

It is right that these forces which prevail in this manner in the human being are hidden from the ordinary person. It is indeed good that a veil is drawn over this, for it is not in the speaking about it that will teach the acolyte and enable him or her to deal with this. Rather, the actual learning is brought about through directly experiencing this. It is this direct experiencing that must be endured once a certain stage of self-confidence and moral strength in the inner life has been attained.

It is for this reason that no true spiritual teacher will give explicit directions as to how to attain to such a higher consciousness stage before the person has reached a definite advanced state of personal integration. The acolyte must have attained three soul qualities; a higher morality, a spiritual presence of mind, and an enhanced self-confidence. These are needed so that through the astonishment that such an experience causes, he or she does not come into danger of losing their own self-sense. {*That is of weakening the ego and thus becoming un-centred*}. Rather, the advanced meditant must be in the state of holding their soul forces firmly around the centre of their ego.

These three capacities are demanded by each spiritual teacher if they are to give instructions as to how to attain to the consciousness stage involved here {*of being actually conscious in the astral world*}. One calls that which is hidden from straight-forward awake day consciousness and which is encountered by the student at this stage, "the Guardian of the Threshold". He guards the threshold because he may not allow the ordinary human being to gaze into that which lurks behind the threshold. {*He is not at first a pleasant sight, as he deliberately embodies, and thereby manifests, the lower self of the meditant*}.

However, this Being essentially loses his unpleasant appearance when the acolyte has attained to the three higher soul qualities mentioned. Earlier, in Atlantean times, in its decadent phase, the leading people, dignitaries in the Mysteries had not bothered to insist that these soul qualities were already intensely developed {*before allowing acolytes to cross the threshold*}. As a consequence, those conditions developed which you know from the description of Atlantis, {*i.e., that caused the destruction of Atlantis*}. This is the second stage {*what has just been described; becoming conscious of the astral plane, and overcoming the lower astral forces in oneself. The first condition or stage of higher consciousness is the experiencing of the thinking-life as central as one's ego itself*}.

The third condition, which is still higher, is achieved by a continuation of the same pathway. Here the meditant is not to be brought into the state of experiencing the realm of thinking as their own, rather they must experience as their own being, as an aspect of their ego, the entire World of Sentiency. {The essential inner nature of} colours, forms, musical tones and also things that are unknown in the physical must now be experienced intimately as one's very own.

{This is a difficult idea to understand, but a conceptual definition of high cosmic consciousness is not easy to achieve. Here this initiate is explaining that to enter into the actual underlying spiritual reality of our feelings, emotions and sensing is to enter into a deeper realm of being than that which underlies logical and insightful (intuitive) thinking. Consider for example, that when one hears a musical note or a series of notes, such as the chromatic or diatonic scale or the interval of "the fifth" that these do have an effect on the soul. One is aware of this effect, even if it is very difficult to verbally define.

Likewise we are aware of the effect of seeing violet or emerald green or seeing a comet moving through the night sky. But we are not really aware of just precisely what this 'effect' is. Certainly one is aware that one feels a definite distinct 'mood' from a certain colour or note, but really this is not acutely conscious. If our ego were to acutely and clearly register the innermost nature of the experience, of our emotive response to the sentient experience, then we would be saying "I" to it, to our world of sentient life experience. We would live fully consciously awake, in this subtle flowing world of sensing and feelings, which is usually semi-conscious.}

{Once the meditant achieves this, then} at this point the ability develops to perceive directly into the higher worlds in normal day-consciousness. {*That is, realms higher than the astral plane, known as Devachan or Spiritland.*} Whilst living in the body, our consciousness is to become one with the divine, higher realities. Hence perception of the aura is acquired, at least as an astral form, if not yet the higher mental-spiritual auras {*which consist of spiritual or Devachanic substance*}.

{We have three auras; it is the soul/astral aura of which most people are really semi-consciously aware. Now at this stage the acolyte actually sees it. This is the beginning of the ultimate goal of spiritual development, continuity of ego-consciousness. But we also have two spiritual auras, one higher than the other, these are the manifestation of the human spirit, or spiritual-body, which has two aspects to it.

These two auras are an expression of our connection to the World of Spirit, also called Devachan, which has a lower and a higher stage.}

If a human being has progressed so far as to consciously perceive in the astral realm, then the meditant has in essence opened a fountain of extraordinary lofty experiences. For then the meditant is able to function with self-awareness in the second state of consciousness - that of dreaming sleep. Such a person is aware of herself or himself and exists quite consciously there just as the ordinary person lives consciously in the physical world.

At the still higher phase, the third phase, the meditant becomes capable of functioning consciously there – in the dreamless sleep phase – where for the ordinary person there is no possibility of conscious existence. But the meditant exists consciously in this realm just as the ordinary person exists in the sense-world, in the normal sense reality. The meditant may thus experience consciously that which was described as the experience of dreamless sleep; he or she experiences the cosmic laws behind Creation; the causative realm of the world.

At this point there is no difference any more between the experiences in so-called unconscious sleep and self-aware day consciousness. This is the 'continuity of consciousness', although this becomes only gradually achieved, step by step. Relatively soon the separating of the soul's threefold powers enables one to live within not only thoughts, but also in sentient experiences, {emotions/feelings}. Then such a person can actually form concepts describing how everything appears. Light on the Path gives the right indications to achieve this high stage. It demands patience, endurance and steadfastness to a very high extent. The possibility for this stage is present as meditation material in the two sentences,

> Before the voice can speak in the presence of the Master, it must have overcome the power to wound.
> Before the soul can stand in the presence of the Master, its feet must be washed in the blood of the heart.

These sentences contain the forces that lead people directly to conscious experience of life as a sentient being. In this way the person can {gradually learn to} say 'I' to the entire world of feelings and sensations. (*See Appendix One for an explanation of the idea of encountering one's sentiency*). The ordinary person says 'I' to their self,[3] however the intuitive person, {*on the first stage of higher awareness*} says 'I' to their thought-life. Those however, who stand on this third step, {*when the second stage of higher consciousness is attained*} wherein one becomes a spiritualized, say 'I' to their world of sentiency, {their experiences of sentiency}. That person is in the condition of experiencing consciously the actual spiritual worlds. That is they can experience all of which you find written in theosophical(-*anthroposophical*) books about 'Devachan'. The facts of Devachan {*the true heavenly realms*} become experiential at this stage.

Do not think that a person who develops to these stages of higher awareness, if it is done in the right manner, becomes a day-dreamer in any way at all. Nor think that they might lose some of their down-to-earth practicality and power of assessing their life circumstances. On the contrary. For them the possibility is gone that they could have any degree of superstitiousness or any sort of dogmatism. Furthermore, on the other side, doubt and scepticism fall from the soul, like scales from the eyes, when the human being achieves at least to some extent the ability to understand what this stage of inner development confers on a person.

There are therefore, two conditions similar to dreaming sleep and dreamless sleep {*that the meditant can achieve, wherein one becomes conscious in both these dynamics*}. When a person can attain to awareness of their experiences in Devachan, then there exists for them still other conditions to which he or she can extend their consciousness. Conditions exist in which she or he can experience something even higher. This something higher is as follows. The meditant learns through his or her faculties in these higher states of spiritual cosmic awareness how the various (archetypal) forms of the universe metamorphose out of each other.

The meditant also learns how a thought-form creates itself, how it comes into being from 'mind-substance' and then envelops itself in astral material. Or how a thought-form from within its own being works from within astral substance and masters it. Further, the meditant learns about the transitional dynamics that occur, where a being directly moves from higher planes down through the astral to the physical plane.

---

[3] That is, to the reciprocal inter-working of their will, emotions and thinking,

The entire sum of the form-metamorphoses that are possible in the universe lie unveiled before his/her gaze, at this stage of higher consciousness. Such a person can give an answer to the question; what shape did a plant have in an epoch long since gone, in order that it may now have its current physical form? {*That is, after the plant realm was cast out of the primal human being.*}

These various metamorphosis-forms throughout the universe, in so far as they belong to our solar system, are revealed at this stage of higher vision. This is called esoterically, "conscious experience of the development of form". {*This indicates that there are various higher realms of Spiritland, and that the meditant can gradually progress to perception of such higher realms. This is cosmic consciousness in its truest form.*}

Furthermore, there is a {further, fourth} phase {of consciousness}, which is analogous to deep dreamless sleep of normal life. This is the condition wherein the person begins to see how Being, how life itself, pours itself into the various life-forms that exist in Creation. Here there is the same difference, but on a higher level, as that between dreaming and deep sleep. It is the difference between the perception of the external form and perception of the various life-modalities {within the form}.

{*This is a fourth stage of esoteric consciousness, beyond just drifting in dreamless sleep. So summing up, there exists then the following four natural states. 1: awake, 2: dreaming sleep, 3: dreamless sleep and also 4: deeply unconscious dreamless sleep. And there are three Phases of Development, also called, Conditions of Development, wherein we have a self-awareness which lifts us up beyond the initial natural state of day-wakefulness;*

1st developmental phase: being conscious in sleep (the 2nd natural state), 2nd developmental phase: being conscious in dreamless sleep (the 3rd natural state); and the 3rd developmental phase: being conscious in deep dreamless sleep (the 4th natural state). To be consciously aware of oneself and of one's spiritual environment in the phase of deep unconscious sleep, is to be functioning in the realm of Higher Devachan.}

It's helpful now to summarize the lecture so far with a brief diagram outlining the stages of consciousness spoken about so far:

4 natural states	the 3 developmental phases of consciousness
awake	= (normal ego-ic consciousness)
dreaming sleep	1: conscious in the dreaming sleep state (astral plane)
dreamless sleep	2: conscious in the dreamless sleep state (lower Spiritland)
deep dreamless sleep	3: conscious in the deep dreamless state (higher Spiritland)

To consider a specific case, {*of the varying degree of perception in higher realms in Spiritland*} the considerable difference is like this. The way you perceive the various spiritual forms in the second stage of these three consciousness stages, is different to how they are perceived in the third stage. Spiritual forms appear at only the second stage in quite different colours to those in the third stage. When you perceive at first a thought-form, in the second stage of consciousness, it then appears to you in radiant yellow tones. There actually exist thought-forms that have this appearance.

Now place yourself in the condition that we call here the third stage. It is now seen that in addition to its archetypal form and colour there is a wonderful 'water-of-life' streaming into the yellow thought-form. The water-of-life can appear for example as a delicate peach blossom colour. (*See Appendix Two for more about the 'water-of-life'*) And you see stationary as well as very mobile forms that transform into each other, but in addition, you see also how from within their inner being these spiritual entities quicken themselves {*i.e. vivify their own life*}.

The result of this ability to transfer your consciousness into these various ethereal forms is that one continually has perception of the laws and dynamics of what we call Devachanic life, but in addition you can make discoveries about these things. You can elucidate from your own higher direct vision, just what previous changes our Earth has undergone during the remote past ages of its so-called Cycles.[4] This vision is however not able to discover such truths concerning other planets in space, at this stage we are considering it is not capable of that.

You perceive in the second phase of consciousness that remarkable metamorphosis which in our literature is designated as something colossal, namely the journey of (or the 'reincarnating' of) the Earth itself through several Aeons of evolutionary conditions. In other words, how our planet went from Higher Devachan to Lower Devachan, then to the astral state, the ethereal state, finally to a physical planet. These transformations of the planet can be directly experienced in this condition, but as already said, only for our planet. It is also possible to learn of the passage of the Earth through the much longer evolutionary phases known as Cycles. This is possible in the third phase, that which correlates to the dreamless deep-sleep stage.

So I have now described for you the consciousness conditions that can be attained through intensive steadfast carrying out of the exercises in 'Light on the Path'. Nevertheless, the student would also need some personal guidance {to attain to these higher stages}. This can only be given when it is certain that the now firmly established inner qualities of acolytes will be continually developed and formed into ever higher kinds. So you see the human being can experience personally some of the teachings of esotericism, once they have undergone an inner preparation. The path leads even further than this, but what those further phases are, I cannot indicate.

Beyond the other side of the high states of awareness described here, there begins that condition of consciousness that strives to make itself entirely non-receptive with regard to the possibility of external sentient life. {*This profound sentence is in fact a fine definition of the misunderstood Buddhist concept of Nirvana, or the state of non-being. Because such a state of consciousness takes one beyond Devachan, and eventually into the realm of Nirvana.*} This enables it to live into a realm situated much deeper in the cosmos. There begins the existence of the Adepts, the great Masters. Only from the experiences

---

[4] The terminology still in use in anthroposophical texts is the confusing Theosophical ones, and I have replaced them, in my research into Steiner's cosmogony. My term, 'Aeons' used here, is actually "Planet" in the traditional terminology, and my term, 'Cycle' is normally 'Round' in Theosophy.

that an Adept can attain is one taken for the first time beyond the boundaries mentioned.

As already said, what I have recounted here only has the purpose of showing in what ways the methods can be found which lead to the spiritual knowledge presented to the world in theosophical books. The purpose of this talk was also to answer the question that occurs in more intimate theosophical circles; "Well, how could you really know about such things?" For to quite some extent the communicating of and reception of such spiritual truths rest on a basis of trust. This has to be so.

However, it can also be required that indications are given regarding from whence this knowledge derives, this spiritual knowledge which we in the western world have been able to again attain. The great spiritual individuals (the Masters) see the possibility that within the theosophical{-*anthroposophical*} movement they can arrange that such teachings are made available. In addition, they can also ensure that those spiritual guidelines are given which when correctly used can assist the development of a corresponding spirituality.

In addition to the significant works of A. P. Sinnett or the 'Secret Doctrine' of H.P. Blavatsky that present such teachings, and which are at the beginning of the Theosophical movement's history; that pearl of wisdom, 'Light on the Path' has also been revealed, which is indeed light on the pathway. Light shall be spread over that pathway which from now, on into the distant future, should be trodden by humanity. If this is trodden or at least understood, only then will one gain some understanding of how this knowledge and the will-power, which should lead us to our spiritual goal, was attained by some, and how it may be attained in the future.

At present the pathway may be accessible to only a small number of people; we do not want to go into this theme tonight. But of this we can be clear, that the One-ness of human experience, where sense-existence ceases and therefore higher experience can begin to appear, requires development of a person's spiritual potential. We can be clear that the experience of the All {*the all-encompassing oneness of Life*} can not be attained other than through a definite developmental process in the spiritual life.

The theosophical movement must attain directly to a deep inner knowledge through the development possibility that is offered in Light on the Path. Spiritual development is offered in a more intensive manner there than in any other method, through its word and teaching and is also spiritually directly in its text. This path to higher knowledge can lead to a great esoteric truth that can be lightly spoken, but only understood with difficulty. A truth that is taught to us in the oldest books of wisdom in the world is contained in these words:

One life lives in all Being;
A unity it is, yet also a multitude;
Just as the Moon reflected on the water
appears in a multitude of images.   *

****

(* *In this lecture Rudolf Steiner was at this early stage of his career, where he was speaking to members of the Theosophical Society, which had its headquarters in Adyar, India. Its members mainly looked towards India for their esoteric ideas. Accordingly, to finish his presentation, he quotes from an ancient Indian sacred text known as the Amritabindu Upanishad.*)

APPENDIX ONE

It is important to add some explanation, as the lecture notes are somewhat fragmentary. The word 'sensation' refers to 'sentiency' and this involves the less consciously experienced, but very alive and potent emotional forces of the soul. However, 'sentiency' also refers to the feelings we experience as we register the external sense-stimuli. This awareness or registering of the environs is brought to us by the senses. However, we also 'sense' various non-physical beings and forces in the other worlds, through the soul. So long as we are incarnate, all such sensing of physical or ethereal things is made possible by the ether body. The ether body, as explained earlier, also mediates to our conscious awareness of sense-stimuli and higher entities, as well as emotions.

So, as beings with a sentient capacity, we have in fact two processes occurring in our inner life. One is awareness of our emotions and moods, the other is that we can sense the physical environment as it impacts upon us, as warmth or sound, etc. (Indeed we also sense invisible energies as well.) So, we could call this twofold sentiency, of being alert to the emotions, as well as to sense-impressions, our feeling life. It is the ether body that makes this possible.

The emotions were described above as potent but less consciously experienced. By this is meant that we are often taken by surprise by our emotions, and we cannot be fully aware of all that our senses are registering. A deeper layer of our being is involved here than thoughts, at least the every-day thoughts which are often only mental images. The less conscious is an aspect of our being, the higher and more remote is the archetypal realm from which it originates.

We are aware of our thoughts, and it is in the first of the higher stages of the mind, that one can enter into the fountain from whence thoughts well up within us. In the second stage, the ego can enter into the less conscious, dream-like feelings in full awareness. Eventually this becomes so clear and real that one can say, "I" to them. And Rudolf Steiner extends this further by stating that the human being can also say "I" to the entire world of Sentiency.}

Thus, to become conscious of, or to say "I" to our will - of which so much is profoundly subconscious in us, would be a still higher stage of clairvoyant consciousness. For the origin of the will is in very remote realms. Whereas the feelings are rather dreamlike in that we are not consciously their creator, the will is even less accessible to the ordinary mind. The will, in its deepest aspect, has its origin in the same realms in which the archetypal 'idea' behind minerals and crystals, the matrix or underlying substance of physical Creation, originates.}

APPENDIX TWO

This expression 'water of life' is the 'Life-spirit'; that is, the archetypal spiritual reality 'behind' the ether energies. It maintains the life of all living things in Creation. In Spiritland, the archetype of all things in all lower realms is perceived. Prana or Ch'i, which is one of ethers, appears here in its archetypal spiritual counterpart, in the third phase of cosmic consciousness, as a stream of beautiful pale mauve energy.

The Initiate uses here the term 'water of life' to connect with the statement of the Cosmos-Spirit that He would give an unquenchable water of life (see Gospel of St. John, Chpt. 4) This refers to the fact that from this Being the archetypal essence of the ethers is present, and is directed into the Earth, and maintained in a vivified state for the future of humanity.

******

Self-Knowledge & The Higher-Self

translated and edited by Dr. Adrian Anderson

A lecture by Rudolf Steiner to members of Theosophical Society, on 16th October 1905, in Berlin.

Themes: Concerning the subtle link between the personal self and the wider spiritual environment; that is, the transcendental reality of the Higher-Self, and the relationship of the Masters to Theosophists (or anthroposophists). What are initiates? Is the so-called 'divine spark' within or without?

Translator's note: In translating this manuscript, I have where necessary expanded the somewhat brief notes taken by a member of the audience. These additional words or phrases of mine, inserted for grammatical reasons, will be placed in brackets. Where more substantial material is needed, e.g., to expand and clarify the meaning of the text, this will be placed in brackets and also italicised *{like this}*. A few sentences have a star (*) after them, and are enclosed in brackets [like these]. This indicates a textual uncertainty, due to poor condition of the original manuscript. It is important to bear in mind that this lecture was given to Theosophists at the turn of the century, early in this great spiritual teacher's career, so it was designed for that context.

Because in this lecture Rudolf Steiner refers to 'initiates' we shall consider this term briefly before the lecture. The initiate, in the contemporary sense, is someone in whom three aspects of the human spirit are further developed than is usually the case. These three elements are designated Manas, Buddhi and Atma in theosophical language; terms which Rudolf Steiner used in his anthroposophical work as well. These three terms refer respectively to the divine-spiritual potential within the soul or astral body, the life-forces (or ether-body) and also the physical body, in which lofty spiritual forces within our will are slumbering. An especially holy and elevated human initiate is Manes, the founder of the Manichean movement early in the 4th century AD, (but very little about this movement is really known, despite recent academic research, for its deeper teachings were kept secret).

His immense task is to help humanity learn to remove evil from the world by bringing to people who manifest hateful deeds compassionate understanding, not hate. Another such person is known as Christian Rosencreutz, the leader of the Rosicrucian movement who seeks to develop humanity towards an inner morality, not a morality based on external precepts. The mysterious post-

Renaissance figure, the Count of St. Germain is a manifestation of Christian Rosencreutz. Rudolf Steiner also refers to the great Persian sage, Zarathustra, who is also known as the Master Jesus, because of his close association with the actual Saviour or divine Jesus who received his higher Self directly from the cosmic Christ, becoming thereby Jesus Christ. This Master seeks to help people on the Path with the more intimate aspects of spiritualising one's being.[5]

The following excerpt from Rudolf Steiner's teachings provides some background information on this subject, which is a prominent theme in the lecture,

> When someone believes that they have nothing to learn from anyone else, then that is a sure sign that such a person is not so advanced. The more advanced a person is, the more certain they become that people are at different levels of development, and that at all times there have been spiritual leaders of humanity. Such initiates are difficult to understand by those less developed, indeed even to be recognised for what they are. However it was from such remarkable persons that the great spiritual stream was poured out in 1875, with the help of the Theosophical movement, this was done because humanity was yearning for this. It is often asked just why such highly developed persons make themselves only slightly perceptible to people.

> The answers lies in one of the deepest books which the Theosophical movement has brought forth, that little booklet which nevertheless encompasses a world of wisdom, 'Light on the Path'. There it is said that these leading individuals who are so far ahead of normal humanity can in fact exist amongst humanity, without being recognised. They can be living in London, St. Petersburg, Berlin and Paris without being recognised, except by a tiny handful, and this is exactly the truth! There are reasons why they must remain hidden. It is necessary that they create a kind of wall around them, so that only those who have lead an appropriate life-style to prepare them for such a meeting, can encounter them.

---

[5] In his esoteric lessons of 1904, 1905 and 1906, Steiner briefly indicated these matters.

It is from such persons that spiritual movements like the Theosophical movement derive. In addition to their infinite goodness they possess a tremendous power, and much that occurs in history proceeds from these persons, without humanity knowing it...the Theosophical Society is only the outer instrument of their work, {it exists} for those men and women who can hear the still, inner voice of the masters' wisdom in quiet moments. It is not important whether the Theosophical Society is rather better or somewhat unsatisfactory, for it is formed in part from human weaknesses and prejudice like all human associations.

The great Masters who have brought us the theosophical wisdom speak to those who permeate with life the Theosophical movement. The Masters do not get involved with external Society matters, they leave that in the hands of those appointed to do this. The external vessel is not so important, but yet we wish to protect it, not because we overestimate it, but because we need it, and because we would be hindered and disturbed in our activity if this external vessel did not exist and encompass Europe, America, Asia, Africa and Australia.[6]

---

[6] From an esoteric lesson in 1904.

Lecture from 16th October 1905:

Self-knowledge and the Higher-Self

Today I wish to speak to you about self-knowledge and knowledge of the divine. These are concepts which can easily be taken up in the wrong way and misunderstood in the context of the spiritual quest. They can also be easily misunderstood experientially by someone on the spiritual path. One reads repeatedly in theosophical books and hears in those popular theosophical lectures or in other lectures in similar movements, that the human being bears within itself the divine Self. And furthermore, that in order to attain to knowledge of God one needs only to let this Self speak. Then the acolyte will find in him or herself the highest knowledge of God. The "Knowledge of the divine Self" has become almost a household expression.

However, just as it is true that for each theosophical gathering there should be as, a guiding maxim, the expression: "Know thy Self", so too it is true that these words can only be understood with the greatest difficulty. Tonight we want to make some effort to understand this expression. This expression "Know yourself" and the other traditional saying, "Self-knowledge is the beginning of spiritual growth" may now sound trivial, but it is equally true that these two expressions must complement each other. I have known people who say in conversation the expression, 'I am the Atma', in me lives the divine Self' or 'In me the divine-human lives' and other such expressions.

Anyone who really wants to penetrate more deeply into an esoteric view of life must completely overcome the trivial understanding of such expressions. Today we want to elucidate the attitude of the esotericist to these expressions. The real esotericist does not speak in this way, and never would his or her words be 'Self-knowledge is knowledge of God.' {*That is, such a phrase is devoid of anything other than abstract prettiness, until one has indeed made it into a reality through spiritual development.*}

But to understand this attitude in the right light, we need to ask 'What can we find in our being actually?' or, 'How much can we learn from our own self?' I will now place at the beginning of this lecture the following precept, from some persons so highly evolved that they have advanced far beyond us all, and from whom we all must learn a great deal. These persons {these higher individuals} say to us about Self-knowledge,

> We learn much from Nature around us; we learn much from the human life around us, we learn things of infinite value from our elder brothers {the Initiates}; but from our own self we learn nothing !

Let us hold this maxim clearly before us. It is the maxim of those who have advanced far ahead in the evolutionary process. Whoever clearly understands what the human being really is, learns to gradually understand these sentences. What is the human being? To answer this we must gaze back upon much that has been discussed in these sessions here. We know that the human being is not something that was born out nothing. It is, as we know, the reincarnation of its earlier personality.

If we consider the human being of today, we have to ask, in what personality was this person incarnate in earlier times? Then we come to a series of incarnations of this person. And when we have gazed back to their very first life on Earth, we are still not at the origin of that person. We only reach back to an older epoch. In that ancient epoch the human being was not yet at all similar to how we appear today, but it certainly existed. Even earlier back we find the human being existing within the deeds and being-ness of the things {and divine beings} of the past.

It is in the events and things of the past that we find the causes of our present existence. When we ask today, "What are we?" we need to answer in this way, "We are today the effect of earlier life-times, of the days we lived in earlier times". When we consider this theme realistically we see that we humans are in essence nothing else than something which has coalesced from the causative factor of our earlier deeds, and the deeds of the World Powers, who have in fact brought together those forces and realities of which we now consist. We are the result of the past, and everything which we can find within us, that has occurred sometime in the past.

What is in us today as personality, was previously deed, was karma; either personal or world-karma, at sometime in the past. We are the expression of this karma. {*Our previous ways of being have become our karma, that is, they have become our current personality. This is a brief description of the working of karma, namely that the predominating deeds or dynamics in the soul-life, and of external actions of a previous life, mould the personality of the next life. I remind the reader that the notes of the lecture are somewhat brief.}*

If we are able to accurately see within our inner being through real self-knowledge, that is by going through the training which the esoteric schools offer, then we find these life-cycles and we find ourselves bonded to the human beings who are all around us. If we also consider what I have spoken here in earlier sessions, then we will know whence we should look to see this matter in another light. Namely that before we existed in our present physical state, we existed in our soul-body as astral beings. *{This is before the Earth condensed into matter from the ether.}*

This part of our being is the sum of our desires and passions; we learnt how, in that ancient past, these were developed, and how they then accommodated themselves to the physical body. What is effective in our physical body is the astral body of the past. This has the desires and passions in itself. And what we see outside ourselves in the various animals - these are the desires which have separated-out from us.

{What existed as part of the soul-life in very ancient humanity, has now become exteriorised and spread out around us as the animal kingdom, which is a kind of tapestry of emotive impulses. There live the desires, lusts and wishes which were part of our soul-life in a remote past of the Earth, when it was an astral-ethereal organism. Of course we did not have the same appearance or mental qualities as we have today. This subject of the remote past evolution of the Earth is described in detail in his book An outline of Esoteric Science. My book, the Rudolf Steiner Handbook, provides a clear description of the basis of these teachings.}

Look at the lions, of these you may say, this lion-nature I once had within me; but I have separated it out from myself, so that I may evolve higher. What exists in me as instinct, from this I have stripped away much, and thus purified my being. I have moulded into a harmonious form these forces in me, but there outside me they exist in the animal kingdom. In the animal kingdom as it surrounds us today, I see my own past astral dynamics.[7]

Now, before I existed as an astral being, I existed as a spiritual being, that is, in a spiritual body. {*In a still more remote cosmic Aeon; remember in all these earlier ages we did not have self-consciousness.*} It was the case that in that remote age also, I separated-off living beings from myself in order to evolve further. In the plant kingdom I now behold the past of my spiritual self {*or Devachanic/mental body.*} The wonderful fruits of the plant kingdom express this past.

{*The forces and beings who were then separated off from the human life-wave and its dynamics on that ethereal primordial planet Earth have become in today's time-cycle, the plant kingdom. These forces were long ago a part of humanity's mental/spiritual being. Indeed even earlier, in the very beginning of the creation of humanity, certain other forces in the primordial planet Earth were separated out from that primeval rudimentary human life-wave. These have become the mineral kingdom of today.*}

Further, when I gaze into the deepest nature of my being, in that which has become intellect and consciousness, then I must perceive that this thinking intelligence, with its images and forms, is reflected in matter as the entire gamut of minerals. Hence the minerals {and crystals} are also an image of my own past. You see we today can comprehend the nature of minerals because we once were this {*so to speak.*} We comprehend the nature of rock crystal because we have separated it out of ourselves. What our intellect {does when it} thinks, had long ago, created the mineral kingdom. {*In other words, through the activity of thinking, humanity long ago created as a kind of by-product the mineral kingdom.*}

{*This sentence completes the section of this lecture which is basically saying that what we have outside us as the realms of nature today, were separated out from us in three remote ages. This first 'separating-out' of forces from the primeval human life-wave, enabled modern humanity to possess later on the fundamental faculty of intelligence, the self-conscious rational mind.*}

---

[7] This is a very brief statement of a central fact of 'spioritual-ecology', that Rudolf Steiner elaborates in many lectures. In this form it is a wonderful sentence for meditation !

Hence we can sense inwardly the significance of the mineral kingdom, and the laws of the physical world, such as those which cause a crystal to form, because this reality is something which humanity once possessed in its own primeval being. This occurred when the planet was a swirling cloud of living ethereal energies, and the focus of divine-spiritual beings whose forces were raying into it, nurturing the growth of the human life-wave throughout remote time-cycles. At that time we did not have a hardened, mineralised body.}

So, in essence, our past lies spread out before us in the world of today; we gaze at our own past evolution when we behold the natural environment around us. Likewise, if there are in our human world souls that are perhaps of lesser evolution, then, in so far as we do this, we are seeing images of our own earlier incarnation, as we were building our later incarnations. The condition of many a person around us is what we ourselves once were. In the ancient past we were not entirely without being, {*even if possessing little consciousness*} and in the future we will have an existence similar to that which deity currently has.* Thus we arrive at an image of the past and of the future. Knowledge of nature is knowledge of our own self, a mirror of the past and of the future, respectively.

(**This sentence in the transcript appears to have become corrupted, and needed additional editorial work.*)

The ancient sage speaks, from the depths of his inner being, that which is really the only clarifying words about self-knowledge. The most wonderful wisdom which the world[8] has ever produced was the Vedanta-wisdom; Tat twam asi - "Thou art that". {*Your own inner self is present also in the external world; and all of this occurs within the being of God*}.[9] There is nothing in the external world that does not belong to our being, to our self. For the external kingdoms of nature are that to which we were once united with our own self. Look at the plants and the animals, all of that is a part of our own self, it was once woven into our self. We belong, together with the past and the future, to one individual being.

---

[8] The Vedanta wisdom, described so highly here, refers to the original ancient wisdom of the Rishis, about 8,000 years ago in the first Post-Atlantean era, of which the current Vedanta texts are an echo,
[9] In the Chandogya Upanishad, this meditative formula is explored; e.g., "He who knows, meditates upon, and realizes this truth of the Self, finds that everything - primal energy, ether, fire water....mind, speech, Scriptures, the entire universe, issues forth from the Self: and thou art that."

Therefore we can say regarding that which is spread out there in space around us, "Thou art that". Self-knowledge does not derive from gazing within, but indeed from gazing out into the surrounding world, with the consciousness that in each being out there, is a part of your own being {*it was a part of one's own inner being in the remote past, and in a sense remains linked to one now*}. The world is not within you, it is spread out there in the great tableau of the universe. The creative God does not speak out of your being, but rather from this great tableau of the universe, {and says}:

> You attain to self-knowledge as you attain knowledge of the world. {This is achieved by} listening to all creatures of Nature, in that you open the senses and spiritual sense-organs for that which the external world speaks to you.

You should not close yourself to the external world, but open the self towards the environment. This you achieve by discarding the normal self in the first instance, and becoming aware that in the external world out there is your true self. Out there is the true self which in the most ancient times had created the mineral kingdom. The stone is the cause of that which is held within you. Feel yourself as one with that which lives and weaves out there. Then feel this same truth in this expression: "Thou art that".

{It could be said that what this passage is denying is in fact also true; that is, that the creator God speaks from within us. But this viewpoint belongs to a different approach to this profound theme - it would then refer to a person becoming initiated, someone in whom the divine - in the form of the Spirit-Self – is indeed beginning to have a tangible presence.

This does not invalidate what is said here. Lectures on such deep subjects have to focus strongly on a particular aspect of these deep life-questions, this does not mean that another perspective is incorrect. For example it is also true to say that for all ennobled, truly striving souls, their future higher spirituality is within them, or at least that it manifests as a special moment of higher ethics and wisdom within us, by raying in from above.}

We human beings belong to the future, not only the past, and we need to work towards the future. To do that, humanity must know something of what it will become in the future. This self which we bear within us, shall in the future become entirely different to what it is today. But that which humanity shall become in the future, that is not in our self, for our self is karma, it is the result of our past. We will in the future become what the self fashions from this. But that we can only learn from those who have progressed on ahead, our 'elder brothers', {the initiates.}

These people are now living a life that is further advanced than ours. For this reason the more highly evolved person says, "I must learn about that which I was and that which I shall become. I can learn much from Nature around me; I learn much from the human life around me, I can learn things of infinite value from my elder brothers (the Initiates); but from my own self I can learn nothing." And such a person means by 'self' the every-day transient self.

{*Note: the now archaic Theosophical expression, 'elder brothers' will from now on be replaced by the term, 'initiates'.*}

We need to comprehend more fully that a deeper self is subtly spread out before us in the world, in so far as its cause lies in the past. Furthermore, the every-day self must learn that its future state exists now in that which the initiates, the wise leaders of humanity, have already experienced and which is a signifier of our own future. We must understand that we cannot contrast self-knowledge with that which the initiates teach, rather that we are to see our future self in these initiates.

Namely, in the sense that what these persons are today, we will become in the future; and should we wish to learn what they in turn shall become, then we need to allow ourselves to be informed about what they have already experienced. In contrast, the minerals, plants and animals cannot tell us about their own being. These shall become in a later time-cycle {approximately} that which we are today.

So we are able to have knowledge about our own self only from those who have attained to the stage that we have yet to reach. Thus we can only sit in humility at the feet of the great leaders of the human race. The wise sages of India say; "The pupil is to be seated in devotion at the feet of the great guru". This does not exclude self-knowledge; on the contrary it includes true self-knowledge, the real self-knowledge.

Consider this, if I am seated at the feet of the great guru, then I may not say, "It is not my will to learn from you, but only from my own self". That would show that one is mistaking the true Higher-Self for something else. The true Higher-Self speaks from all beings. Hence from the words of the initiate, my self also speaks to me. For the true Higher-Self also speaks to us from the wisdom of my guru.

{Note also, the word "guru" here for students of Rudolf Steiner becomes changed as to its meaning: it means an advisor, not an authority figure who must be obeyed. The Oriental guru-acolyte relationship is not recommended by, and is not part of, the spiritual path established by Rudolf Steiner, and elucidated in his books. But members of the Theosophical Society were then closely involved in Indian spirituality. Hence Steiner used a term which was meaningful to his audience. In 1904 it was still eight years before the Anthroposophical Society was founded in which he draws on western leitmotifs and imagery.}

It is grey theory to say that one need only let the true self speak. Whereas it is a genuine esoteric activity when one harkens to the initiates of humanity. That which we are, and which our true self has to say, speaks to us the best from initiate, or from a book such as Light on the Path. In the eternal sentences which you find in this book or in the New Testament, especially in the Gospel of St. John or in the sacred writings of the great Masters. In such sources, your Self speaks to you, as it also does when you are at the feet of the guru; tranquil and at peace with what you now are, as result of the past. Such a master needs only to be somewhat more advanced than you, then there resounds your own Self in your ears, in your soul, instructing you.

{Rudolf Steiner's own anthroposophical text 'Theosophy' which was at this time had just been published, is to be included in this category. And his book 'An Outline of Esoteric Science' (not published for 6 years) is also included in this category. In fact he commented that this book arose through a co-operative working some high initiate 'colleagues' of his in higher worlds. And naturally Rudolf Steiner's vast output of lectures also belong here as well.}

And if you encounter a meditative saying, as is found here (in Light on the Path), such as "Expect the blossoming of the flower after the blustering storm, not earlier." then {*it is rightly understood if one concludes*}, 'this is a saying of a Master who has long ago been through the stage where I now am, and who can instruct me about my own self'. Therefore the esotericist says, 'above all I should deeply engage myself in what the wise leaders of humanity have offered to us'. From this the esotericist will gradually attain humility and also tranquillity. An initial step towards this goal is to listen to what the great individualities who have appeared in the course of history have to say to us, people in all the various fields of knowledge, who are wiser than ourselves.

We look to the great artists and to the great wise leaders of humanity, in so far as these are noted in exoteric history. When we allow a painting by Raphael to influence our soul, or when we read the great works of Plato about the immortality of the soul, or let his Phaeton permeate the soul, then our own Self is speaking to us. Or when we absorb the writings of Johann G. Fichte and similar people, our Self speaks to us, we take the first step up to a higher element of our own self.

Then, when we have absorbed what is given at this stage, at least partially, we can approach those deep writings, the authors of which are unknown, because the personal name was considered unimportant. For example the book, Light on the Path which derives from a great wise leader of humanity, was only written down {*in the manner of a scribe*} by Mabel Collins; she was just the instrument for this process. In like manner our true Self speaks to us through the Gospels, through the 'The Bhagavad Gita', and through other ancient texts of humanity. {*He elsewhere included 'The Imitation of Christ' amongst these texts. But to students of Steiner today, Rudolf Steiner's own teachings, which at this time were only just becoming known, are included in this category, and have a greater value than most earlier inspirational texts.*} In all of these our own true Self is speaking, which we thus find most effectively, by searching not within but without. As the old Vedanta wisdom says; "Thou art that".

Then when we no longer detect in us that we no longer wish to say something, but now simply yearn to be a vessel {for wisdom}, and have surrendered all of our narrow personal-self qualities, then higher individuals may speak to us. But for this to occur, there is still much more that we must achieve. Above all things, a more thorough consideration of the precept, 'It is with Self-Knowledge, knowledge of our so-called inner nature, that the will develops for perfecting of one's being'. This is also recognition of the fact that through our normal self we can learn nothing. For truly, through this personal self the human being surrenders itself to the most difficult illusions.

What is this true self? Consider it more closely. Is it to be found in our external life, our daily activities? Are you this self, when you go to the meal-table? Are you it, when you go about your daily work? Clear self-knowledge shall say to you, "no, this is not the case", for it is the normal natural personality and natural urges which are active then. One is carried along and impelled {*not compelled*} by the personality. Natural urges and drives which have also fashioned the physical body, push and press on your inner being. It is the greatest illusion when someone says, "I am eating", or "I am going for a walk" or "I am taking care of this or that business activity". For then one is not the cause of the action, but one is driven by something.

For the person who immerses themselves in self-knowledge {*by going within*} the normal inner life is not the source of Truth. Such a meditant does not find the real self within, rather one notices that one finds in the self, forces which derive from the external world. These forces are experienced as pressing and pushing on one's inner life. Indeed even when you are very strongly interconnected with your present individuality, what are you?

You are the result of your karmic development from earlier times. In other words, that which we in this life think and feel, we do so think and feel because we were driven in an earlier life to this or that inner activity. The earlier lives have an influence throughout our current life. If you ask, with some self-knowledge why I do this or that, you do not come in this way to your true Self, rather to the earlier causative factors in the life-cycles.

If you still further test yourself as to what you have acquired inwardly in this present life, you find the same thing. Take for example the faculty of speech. Is speech your self? You speak; you believe that you yourself are speaking. But can the human being speak from out of her or his self? If the answer were, 'yes', then each human being would have to be able to form new words. That is each person would have to bring forth speech out of her or his own self each time. But the language **itself** speaks, the language of the nation, that is. The entire nation speaks through the language, the entire nation is our own language-basis, and speaks to us, and through us.

{*Summing up this point; Even our faculty of speech, from this point of view, could be considered as deriving from external forces rather than our innermost being, namely from our ethnic group or national folk-*

soul. If our speech were really fully our own innermost self in manifestation, then each human being would have to have his/her own unique language. So, here too, we are the impelled, not the impeller. Only when we see our personal self as existing external to us, present in the environment, and forming us from without, do we really have self-knowledge}.

We can push on ever further towards self-knowledge, but we will find that the Self moves ever further ahead of us. When we understand, "Tat twam asi" we will thereby see that this self is spread out, poured out, over the external world; then we will be living in Self-knowledge. But one must be quite clear about, and have at some time felt inwardly, what it means to be hollowed-out this in way and to so stand before one's own self. The person who has attained to this self-knowledge will experience her or his own being as if hollowed-out. If we wish to attain the goal of Self-knowledge we must first experience a desolation and darkness within our being.

There where formerly we experienced warmth, we now sense through self-knowledge that this warmth does not stream from our heart, but rather that it was first poured into the external world, and that our self is only the confluence of forces from the external world. At the place of each arrogant feeling of selfhood, there is now the fullest humility and the knowledge that we are of little account relative to the wide world. {*The student in this process must have sufficient maturity to know that all of the above teaching does not seek to change one's own integrity and self-respect.*}

{*At this point in the lecture it may be helpful to summarise: in order to comprehend the normal self, one needs to be able to recognize in the interplay of general elemental forces in the environment, the matrix, the source of one's inner life. Only then is there understanding of the current 'self', the personality. One could call this insight, 'self-knowledge', whereas in contrast one could call understanding of and union with the Higher-Self, 'Self-knowledge'. This is an important distinction which now needs to be clarified. Spirituality could be defined as the union of the personality with the Higher-Self; this is Self-knowledge or union with the true Self. But before this can occur, there has to be personal growth which involves knowledge of the normal self.*

This knowledge consists in the normal exoteric world, of comprehension of one's negative and positive qualities, one's strengths and weaknesses. But esoterically this self-knowledge entails comprehending how the external world, the realms of Nature, are present in a certain way in our own human nature, forming the normal somewhat illusory self. It is this second aspect of the normal self and so-called self-knowledge that is presented in this lecture, together with some aspects of the Higher-Self-knowledge as a second theme.}

Desolate, dry and hollowed-out is the result of that self-knowledge which wills to seek only within the current self. But once we have attained to this and understand that our self is to be found entirely in the external world, then we have developed sufficiently to allow the teachings of the initiates to speak to us, the Keepers of the Seal of our Higher-Self.[10] They may then speak to us, once we no longer want our Higher-Self to be in effect us, as we now are. {*When we no longer want to identify our Higher-Self with our current personality.*}

Our lower self is outside, spread across the various levels of natural existence, and our Higher-Self is also arrayed outside us, in those who have developed further than we have. Self-Knowledge is knowledge of the world, and the beginning of self-knowledge is that our Self must stream into us from outside. {*In later years, especially in 1924, Steiner unveiled precise and profound teachings concerning the interconnectedness of our Higher-Self to the various sublime beings of the Hierarchies, and not just to Initiates. He thereby gave real substance to the general idea that 'we are from God', via the hierarchies.*}

No-one can tread the Path and feel the precept, 'Go within, that is the Path you should seek' without being driven to another guiding precept, 'Seek boldly the way up, out of yourself'. True Self-knowledge begins when we no longer seek within, but instead with humility seek in the external world. Then something of the future is revealed to us, of that which has not yet come to be. In fact there are such persons as have the ability, because of their advanced development, to see already that which our own self in the future will see.

{*These seers perceive the evolutionary journey of the human life-wave, from the heights of the spirit, gradually down the lesser realms into physical existence, and they perceive how in the future the journey will be an ascent.*} We have journeyed through the astral realm, through the spiritual realm, and we will again struggle upwards into and through these realms in the future, after going

---

[10] See Appendix about this phrase.

through the physical world. In order to raise oneself up to the higher worlds, we need firstly to develop the inner strength, {to make such an ascent in consciousness.}

These higher worlds are on the other side of the threshold, where we go after death. These realms can be perceived by the initiates. For one who has in humility attained to the stage of Initiation can perceive these realms already during life. That is, those realms which the human being enters when he or she has gone through the gate of Death. How does the seeker learn to gaze into such realms? Not by brooding upon oneself, but through carefully listening to that which the initiates teach.

For example, through comprehending the statement that self-knowledge is present when one listens carefully to the guidance of the initiates. In the teachings of an initiate are forces which awaken the spiritual eyes and ears in our own astral and spiritual bodies, "In that a master speaks to me, forces stream into me which awaken in me spiritual eyes and ears through which I myself can learn to see into those realms to which an initiate has access".

I should no longer will to use {as a basis for the Quest} that which is in me, which is only the effect of the past; rather I should hollow out my personal-egoistical nature and become an empty vessel for the wisdom of the initiates. Only after this is attained may I receive the wisdom which allows me to gaze into the future of humanity. So, for the seeker Self-knowledge is living existentially in a humble listening to those who have already learnt what she or he has still to learn, and this of course will normally be the case for the student. It is for this reason that the esotericist reveres any true initiate or advanced disciple on the path, if such are encountered, and does not seek to find the Master or advanced disciple within himself or her self, but rather finds the self in the other, greater self which is outside there in the world.

So, for the esotericist self-knowledge means devotion to an advanced disciple on the path or a Master, and seeking the greater self externally, namely within the Master. Such an attitude also conforms to the precept, "Thou art that". It would be lack of humility in the strongest sense, to say that one can 'find within' that which the initiates teach us. [11]

For this reason one becomes humble after just a little progress has been made. For this reason too, from a certain point in the Path onwards, one becomes far less ready to declare one's own opinion. For what is this opinion? Simply a result of past destiny. When one is present in a situation and suppresses the urge to be giving an opinion, even when one believes one is called upon to speak, and yet remains silent, listening to those who have advanced beyond our stage, we gain much. By such listening intently to what resounds towards us from the environment, we earn the right to really be heard. Indeed even the simple person, who knows how to live in this way, will have much that is deep and beautiful.

Whereas if you encounter someone who only wants to express his opinion, that person will have little of value to say. On the other hand, if someone speaks sincerely about primal truths deriving from those persons who are wiser than himself, then his or her words will have infinite value, even if the words are apparently quite simple. Providing that he/she speaks really from his/her own individuality, and has some awareness of the meaning of these truths.

The deepest wisdom resounds from the deepest humility and modesty. Those people who have already in previous times spoken the highest truths, they spoke in a different manner to those who today are so often declaring their views, saying, 'this is what I think' or 'I believe its like this', or 'this is my standpoint'. Those people who have evolved further towards wisdom don't speak like that. They refer to those other wiser people whose attitude they respect, for they know that their own opinion is worthless.

Those persons who have founded the Theosophical Movement, those who represent this movement in the right way, have always referred to. and relied upon. the great Individuals who stand behind them.

---

[11] The reader must be careful to not confuse this with a feeling of familiarity, of inward knowing, of esoteric truths such as this book contains. This is a different phenomenon, and derives from the fact that in the 16 -19th centuries some millions of souls, in the time before descent to a new birth, were given a special instruction in the spiritual truths needed in modern times, and also in the dangers of technological materialism. The archangel Michael was and is the regent of this 'schooling' process.

These founders regarded such initiates {as an aspect of} the true Higher-Self, speaking through them. The Masters are therefore our own Higher-Self {*in a certain sense*}. The words of the living Masters, quite apart from ourselves, impart the actual wisdom-filled activity to the Theosophical movement. They freely offer their will, and make themselves into instruments of the movement, for that is their conviction.

Their preference regarding our behaviour in this matter is, for us when we are in the presence of someone else, to be able can say, 'there is nothing in me, nothing should resound from me, for I will make myself into an empty vessel, from which the master speaks'. But the master should not be regarded as one's own self, rather this "higher-self" should be {that is, remain} the wise leader, a brother of all humanity. Someone who lives alongside us, just as we live, and whose words we hear and want to understand in the right way, namely:

> We learn much from Nature around us; we learn much from the human life around us, we learn things of infinite value from the Initiates; but from our own self we learn nothing.

For we are, in our current existence {as a personal self} only a transit-point[12], a section of a passageway; and we can and shall attain nothing if we seek to make this current transit-point the essential thing of our existence.[13] For then nothing would occur in the world through our own being, except what we have already done. You would be an infertile fruit on the human tree of life. For everything of which you are capable has already happened, if you remain with your own normal self. Only once you make the personal self fertile and creative by the higher-self, which exists in the world, can you bring something new into the world.

Then from your inner being an activity occurs which does not only have the past with its effects within it. Indeed the only way at all for us to have the power to bring about something really new and

---

[12] In German, the phrase is „wir sind nur ein Durchgangspunkt.."

[13] A closer translation here of "den Wirksamen" which I have translated as 'the essential thing' is the scholarly expression, 'The efficacious (formative) reality'. Further this sentence is not denying that a divine spiritual reality is part of every human being's nature. Rather it is saying that the spiritual 'spark' is normally outside the functioning personality; it is not integrated into and efficacious within it.

productively creative is to have a connection with whatever occurs in the world that is actually higher than ourselves. It is solely through this connection {*to an inspired activity which transcends our normal abilities,*} and the fully humble consciousness we have discussed earlier, that we can have this creative power.

And this decision, to seek union out of the emptiness of the personal self with that in our world which is higher than ourselves is the first step towards being a student of the spiritual path. Whoever does not will to become their own Higher-Self, so to speak, can never become an acolyte in the esoteric sense, a student on the path to initiation. It is this alone which gives us the power to learn something in the world, for without this consciousness we are nothing, we are devoid of power and might.

All true esoteric schools have expressed the above consciousness as a full reality, in two sentences, which when a person wants to really live them each moment of his or her life, and not just take them abstractly, gives the soul a tremendous empowerment, as only a human being can attain. All esotericism and all human striving is encompassed in these two sentences, which we soon focus on. But note that they must so be lived that with each step of our life they pulse through us, permeating us so that we do nothing without awareness of these two sentences, which basically harmonise with each other.

> Everything around about us is there for us. And we ourselves are there for God.

What exists around about us, has merged into us and has brought us to the present standpoint. Here we are and we gaze out at everything which is out there around us. This displays to us our own past, you can find nothing else within your inner being. The first sentence indicates that in your own astral body you can find that which is spread out around you as the sentient feelings of the animal kingdom. Everything which is sentient in Nature is a reflection of what lives in your astral body.

{*In other words, everything living in the world which is sentient, is a mirror of our astral body. This means the animal/insect realms and the nature spirits; they depict the matrix of emotions and sensory responses from which the human sentiency has evolved, and to which it still has deep interconnectedness. This sentence also implies in the light of the preceding pages, that everything which has ethereal life-energies within it is a mirror of our ether-body. That is to say, our human ethereal-body or life-force organism has its original matrix and current interdependency with the plant kingdom and less evolved nature spirits. There is a symbiotic link between them.}*

What is around us as stone and minerals is a reflection of what exists in our physical body.[14] However our ego {self} is empty, {*i.e. it is devoid of reflections from the environment*}. If you want to have content in the ego, which can be found reflected in the environment, then you must gaze into the future, not upon that which is of the past. But then you must be aware that in the bridge between these, something of importance comes to expression. Namely that between these two, the past and the future, you yourself are the focus, for only you can be the bridge between what you have so far developed and that which will develop.

For what we can see as a reflection of our self in Nature, that is what we once were. But by following the guidance of the initiate, we can actually learn to observe what we shall see around us in the future, {*that is, in the future we shall have a more 'inwardly-real' self, and, after some time, this new element of our being will have its reflection somehow, in our future environment*}. This still-to-be-attained real Self is in fact now formatively moulding us towards the future. In this way does a person who has understood these matters look into the world. Such a person says, all this has happened in the past, and occurs now, for my sake, namely that I could arise into being. All that I perceive in my environment belongs to this reality.

If someone were to take anything out of this world around you, then you would not be the same as you now are, for all this had to be, in order that you could exist as you are. Just as a house is built upon layers of stones, so too are the various elements of nature there. In order that the upper storeys are built, the lower ones must first be

---

[14] Furthermore, this sentence is saying that everything in the mineral kingdom (soil, rocks and crystals) is a reflection of our physical body. This is somewhat self-explanatory, but bear in mind that in the initiation wisdom revealed by Rudolf Steiner all such statements have a deeper meaning. In this case, the various especial qualities in minerals have paradoxically their origin in the distant zodiac stars. For example, the Capricorn forces have formed the knees in our body, as well as the gem, olivine/peridot, (described by him as 'chaste and pure.) Whereas the Taurean forces for example have formed our larynx as well as the lovely gem, aquamarine.

built, and if one were to take out just one stone, the house would no longer look right. It is the same with people, if one of the stones, that is, elements that have built us up were to be removed, we would not have the same appearance. One does not grasp this idea straight away, but as the student of yoga would say, through meditative yogic exercises, one learns to understand this idea.

{Understanding of these larger evolutionary matters may be helped by considering how we appear as soul and spirit to the seer. That is by a consideration of the more easily understood matter of our auras, the soul or astral aura and the higher of the two spiritual auras. Our higher spiritual-organism is at this stage of our evolution somewhat tenuous, somewhat lacking definition and inner substance.

It must first be filled, from outside of our personal being, with that which is living as humanity's future spiritual potential. The astral body is filled with forces and a variety of intensely coloured forms, from its long history of lifetimes on the Earth. Whereas the higher spiritual body is perceived only as a pale ovoid form of indigo and greenish quality, with little specific content interpenetrating the astral aura.}

If we gaze out into the world, we see what is around us there, whereas if we look into our own self and what it will become, we find the newly forming buds of future fruits. Then it becomes clear to us that we do not exist here for our own sake, but so that we may become as the initiates are; that we are in effect emulating them in our striving. We need to strive towards real examples, rather than be influenced by affected, artificial ideas. We need to live in the reality, not in abstractions.

That is the meaning of the second sentence. In this way the divine develops within humanity, in that we find the connection to that which is for us the present, and what is our potential for the future. It is the will of the Divine that we are here; it is not for our own self. The person who understands these two sentences thinks in this way, rather than thinking of her/his personal self. One contemplates what exists in the world environment because of one's own normal self, and that one is here now so that the future may come into being. From these two points of view, there flows the power to become effective not for oneself, but for the Divine which is evolving itself out of us. These are the two pillars of all esoteric reality.

If you will to ascend up to higher sources of wisdom, then you must live under the auspices of these two sentences, they must pulse through and en-soul everything in your life. You must become intimately acquainted with these two sentences. In them are concentrated the intention of our deliberations today, they should be present in letters of gold in the mind of every student of esoteric wisdom. Letters which however speak only to those souls who are as if emptied out {*of personal egotism*}, for they appear as if erased, when someone with selfishness or egotism wishes to gaze at them. If someone wills to approach the portals of the mystery school with complete selflessness, then he or she sees these two pillars of all true Knowledge:

> Everything around about us is there for us. And we ourselves are there for God.

These are the two precepts which empower the esotericist, once they have been fully understood. We need to really will to learn just what is around about us, and when someone asks us about our Higher-Self, we need to indicate that it is something beyond our own personal being, yet not in an uncertain abstract way, but as a concrete reality. It is precisely in this way that I intended to speak to you today.

For when such matters are understood, one also understands that the Theosophical movement is not possible without an esoteric foundation, without the knowledge of the Masters, and without knowledge of the higher worlds. These higher realms are our own future. What we are doing today works into our astral body, and upon this the future world shall be built. There are souls who have worked more upon their astral bodies than we have, and they present existentially to us the images of our own Higher-Self.

If we live under the influence of such knowledge, then we can deal with all the difficulties which we encounter from outside. Usually, such difficulties derive from ordinary people, not from the initiates, and one comes to understand gradually, that the mistakes of such a great movement, such as that of the Theosophical stream, do not derive from this stream, but are carried into it from outside. What kind of movement is the Theosophical movement? It comes into being when a number of people are brought together and when through their souls flows the life of holiness and the wisdom of the Masters. Once they have come together, this life may flow through them. But they come to this movement from outside it, from all walks of life, and bring their short-comings with them.

Such imperfections are not immediately dispensed with, so they must manifest within the movement. These defects do not however derive from the movement, rather they are brought into the movement. Hence when uncivil matters occur, these are not something that exists within the movement, but rather they are something which is external to it. We have to be clear that severe crises could be ahead, and we must carry the imperfections of those people who join us. This is the attitude needed when looking at what happens in our movement. There is much to criticise in we all do, however we have entered into it from outside and still have the imperfections of the external world. But, let us be clear that through {*ongoing self-development which is facilitated by*} the Theosophical-(anthroposophical) movement we must put aside these imperfections.

Even those who may be the most valuable members also need to strive to put aside their imperfections. It is actually a defect to refer to the defects of others. We need to search out the imperfections in our own being, and when there is greatness and nobleness outside us in the spiritual powers behind the movement, then we have in the Theosophical* movement the right [*vessel for our own future development."*]

{{*I have added these last words, because the lecture transcript breaks off, just at the end of the lecture.*}}

* The Anthroposophical movement is a more accurate way to understand these words, in view of the fact that Rudolf Steiner was no longer welcome in the Theosophical Society after 1912.}

****

APPENDIX

The Keepers of the Seal of our Higher-Self

This remarkable expression, in German, 'die Siegelbewahrer unseres hoheren Selbstes' is full of allusion to the initiation terminology from the wholesome Gnostics of the Hellenistic Age, and is a meditation in itself. It appears to mean that the Initiates are in effect those who hold the key that opens up our access to our own Higher Self; they are actively seeking to help the acolyte move towards self-initiation. In the Gnostic wisdom there is to be found knowledge of various spiritual beings who monitor the progress of souls towards higher consciousness. The soul needs a seal to open up the way into each of the spiritual realms. These beings also monitor the progress of the souls of the dead as they progress upwards through the various planes.

www.ingramcontent.com/pod-product-compliance
Lightning Source LLC
LaVergne TN
LVHW061217060426
835507LV00016B/1978